Little Bits of JOY

Little Bits of JOY

Paloma Spaulding

This publication is meant as a source of valuable information for the reader, however, it is not meant as a substitute for direct expert assistance. If such a level of assistance is required, the services of a competent professional should be sought.

Copyright © 2022 by Paloma Spaulding

All rights reserved. No part of this book may be reproduced or transmitted in any form or by any means, electronic or mechanical, including photocopying, recording, or any information storage and retrieval system, without permission in writing from the author.

ISBN: 978-1-6653-0390-3

This ISBN is the property of BookLogix for the express purpose of sales and distribution of this title. The content of this book is the property of the copyright holder only. BookLogix does not hold any ownership of the content of this book and is not liable in any way for the materials contained within. The views and opinions expressed in this book are the property of the Author/Copyright holder, and do not necessarily reflect those of BookLogix.

1 1 2 1 2 2

☉This paper meets the requirements of ANSI/NISO Z39.48-1992 (Permanence of Paper)

Images courtesy of Adobe Stock

Introduction

Little Bits of Joy was inspired by a daily, morning routine with my dear friend and sorority sister ("My Sands!"), Dr. Fara Bostic. We were both laid off, so we cheered each other up with a daily morning moment of prayer, inspiration, and motivation. That is when the first "little bit of joy" about oatmeal was discovered. We realized then, that there were many "book worthy" *Little Bits of Joy* that helped us make it through the week that would cheer up many who needed some light inspiration. This book would complete a set of mini-books I was writing. We also decided future *Little Bits of Joy* could have different themes going forward. Look forward to hers about the journey toward obtaining a PhD.

This book was started around 2016, long before events that have amplified the need for *any*thing that will make us smile. So, recently, I added the WWFD (What Would Fara Do?) section as an additional list of really simple things you can do right away to put some joy in your day (without downloading another app or paying for another service).

Please enjoy reading my little bits of joy that have brightened up my environment, soothed a frustrating day, or helped me improve someone else's.

REMEMBERING YOU HAVE SOME CRANBERRIES, CINNAMON, AND NUTS TO LIVEN UP YOUR BLAND OATMEAL FOR BREAKFAST

TREATING YOURSELF TO A SEASHELL TEACUP THAT REMINDS YOU OF A GREAT BEACH VACATION

A BREAKFAST TREAT THAT
REMINDS YOU OF YOUR
"FUTURE" BED-AND-BREAKFAST
PLACE IN MEXICO ...
*"**QUE RRRICO!!**"*

FINDING OUT YOUR FAVORITE NEIGHBOR HAS EVEN MORE FESTIVE PARTY-HOUSEWARES THAN YOU SO NOW YOU CAN PLAN EXCUSES TO *USE THEM*

DISCOVERING YOUR FELLOW "SEPTEMBER-BABY" NEIGHBOR IS ALSO INTO CRYSTALS SO DOESN'T THINK YOU'RE JUST A CRAZY FLOWER CHILD

LONG-DISTANCE COCKTAILS WITH YOUR FAVORITE HAPPY HOUR BUDDY WHO MOVED OUT OF STATE... *KLINK!*

SHARING A NICE POT OF TEA WITH A FRIEND, USING THE TEA SET THAT WAS COLLECTING DUST IN THE CHINA CABINET

HAVING A FRIEND THAT ALWAYS SAYS JUST WHAT YOU'RE THINKING AND SEEMS TO COMPLETE YOU!

ENJOYING THE LAST NIGHT OF SUMMER AT THE CONDO POOL WITH FRIENDS AND A BOTTLE OF CHAMPAGNE!

A FRIEND THAT MAKES YOU FEEL LIKE A WEALTH OF POSITIVITY, CREATIVITY, AND KNOWLEDGE EVERY TIME SHE CALLS FOR A CHAT

BEING CALLED EFFERVESCENT BY ONE FRIEND, THEN HAVING ANOTHER FRIEND COMPARE YOU TO THE "POP" OF A CHAMPAGNE BOTTLE YEARS LATER

MISSING A REUNION BUT FEELING LOVED, MISSED, AND INCLUDED THANKS TO HIGH TECHNOLOGY

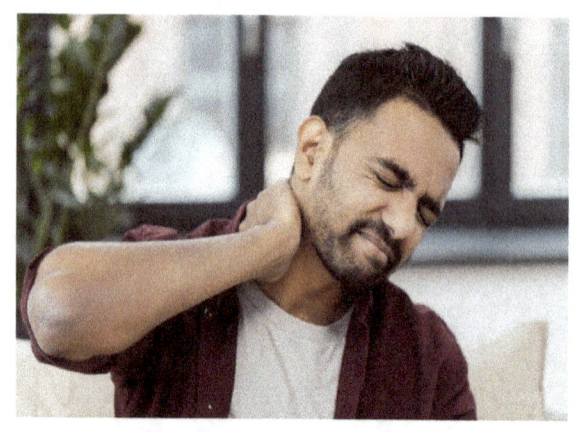

FINDING OUT THAT EVEN YOUR FRIENDS YOUNGER THAN FIFTY, CAN RELATE TO EXPERIENCES IN ***THE 50th DIMENSION!***

FINALLY FINDING AN AIR FRESHENER FOR THE HOUSE THAT DOESN'T PUT YOU *"OUT OF THE HOUSE"*

A VIBRANT, NEW BEDDING SET THAT EASES CABIN FEVER AND STRESS: SMOOTH, FRESH SHEETS, AN AIRY COMFORTER, A FLUFFY MATTRESS PAD, AND PILLOWS THAT DON'T PUT A CRICK IN YOUR NECK!

REALIZING THAT "SPRING WATER" SOAP BARS MAKE YOUR LINEN CLOSET SMELL LIKE GOOD SACHETS—*HA!*

SEEING YOUR FAVORITE PLANTS
COME BACK TO LIFE AFTER YOU
THOUGHT AN EARLY FREEZE
KILLED THEM FOR GOOD

FINALLY!! FINDING YOUR FAVORITE, SPORTY, EXPENSIVE PRESCRIPTION GLASSES WHILE CLEANING UP BEHIND FURNITURE!

REMEMBERING THE PASSWORD
TO YOUR HIDDEN LOCKBOX KEY
WHEN YOU LOCK YOURSELF
OUT OF THE HOUSE . . . *AGAIN!!!*

CALLING A FRIEND EARLIER THAN USUAL—ONLY TO FIND OUT SHE WAS JUST THINKING SHE NEEDED YOUR ADVICE

REMEMBERING TO CALL A DEAR FRIEND *EXACTLY ON* HER BIRTHDAY... INSTEAD OF SOMETIME THAT MONTH!

SEEING YOUR SPOUSE'S CAR COME HOME EARLY WHEN YOU HAPPENED TO LOOK OUT OF THE FRONT WINDOW:

YAYYYY, HAPPY HOUR!!!

FINDING YOUR HUSBAND PREPPING THE PATIO FOR A GOOD PRESSURE WASH:

LIGHT UP THE GRILL!!

YOGA REVELATIONS: I CAN GET UP AND DOWN WITHOUT MAKING "THAT NOISE" BECAUSE I FINALLY DID MY FAVORITE YOGA ROUTINES THIS WEEK

NOTICING THAT A *LITTLE* CARDIO EVERY WEEK, CAN GET RID OF A *LOT* OF JOINT ACHINESS EVERY DAY

FINDING AN URGENT CARE PLACE *THAT TAKES APPOINTMENTS!!!* INSTEAD OF WAITING ALL NIGHT AT THE EMERGENCY ROOM WITH YOUR NINETY-YEAR-OLD MOM

EVERYONE GETTING CHRISTMAS GIFTS DURING YOUR UNCLE'S NINETIETH BIRTHDAY PARTY ... BECAUSE THAT'S THE KIND OF FAMILY YOU HAVE!

REALIZING THAT THOUGH YOUR PARENTS MAY BE LOSING THEIR STRENGTH, THEY'RE GAINING MORE QUALITY TIME WITH YOU AS AN ADULT

A NICE, CALMING DENTIST WHO TREATS YOUR TEETH THE WAY MICHELANGELO TREATED MARBLE

A POWER-CONTROLLED CAR SEAT YOU DON'T HAVE TO KEEP CHANGING TO YOUR MUNCHKIN-SIZED SETTINGS EVERY TIME YOU GET IN THE DANG CAR

REALIZING THAT ALTHOUGH
YOU JUST LOST YOUR JOB, YOU
JUST GAINED CONTROL OF EVERY
HOUR OF EACH DAY UNTIL YOU
GET ANOTHER ONE... *HA!*

TAKING A REAL NAP... ON PURPOSE... WITH THE TV OFF *AND* THE PHONE OFF... BECAUSE YOU *FINALLY* LET YOURSELF RELAX

FINDING OUT THERE'S A *MURDER, SHE WROTE* MARATHON ON A COLD, DREARY, POPCORN-AND-MIMOSA DAY

COMPLETING YOUR SMALL BUSINESS PLANS AND PAPERWORK *YOURSELF* AFTER ALL THE FOLKS "HELPING YOU" LET YOU DOWN

GETTING SIX MORE CUSTOMERS DOING YOUR "IN-BETWEEN-JOBS" JOB BECAUSE YOUR NEIGHBORS SAW WHAT GOOD WORK YOU DID FOR SOMEONE ELSE!

THE MOMENTUM YOU GET FROM FINISHING THAT *BORING, TEDIOUS* TASK YOU DREADED STARTING IN THE FIRST PLACE

HAVING THE ENERGY TO FINISH YOUR WHOLE TO-DO LIST THANKS TO A STRONG, HOMEMADE LATTE WITH BREAKFAST!

SEEING YOUR FAVORITE CHOCOLATE-CANDY KIOSK AT THE MALL BECAUSE THERE'S NO STORE LOCATION WHERE YOU LIVE NOW

FINDING AND LAUGHING WITH PEOPLE AS SILLY AS YOU ARE ABOUT YOUR DOG DURING A... ***RUFF*** YEAR

GOD SHOWING UP WHEN YOU LEAST EXPECT IT: PROVIDING A PATH FROM THE DARKEST NIGHT TO THE BRIGHTEST DAY

KNOWING YOUR OWN
CREATIONS ARE APPRECIATED,
LOVED, AND LAUGHED AT BY
MORE THAN JUST YOUR
FELLOW MEMBERS OF
THE 50th DIMENSION

WWFD

This section is dedicated to that dear friend, Fara, that inspired this *Little Bits of Joy* book we hope becomes a series. I call this section "What would Fara do?"

Fara has a flair for the elegant and festive from being raised in a fabulous area of Southern California. However, she is as down to earth and caring as she is fabulous. She freely shares that flair through her simple yet creative ideas and gifts. I noticed that some of that flair was for making the fabulous out of the ordinary you can find already in your house. I was raised in Berkeley, California so my flair has a flower-child touch you'll see in my WWFD list.

- Use antique or decorative knobs to replace old furniture hardware.
- Decorate your closet walls or door interior with a framed picture.

- 🕊 Make a coffee station out of your favorite kitchen items: festive mugs, jars, and decorative teacups. They're perfect for coffee, beverage pods, and coffee condiments!

- Include in your Christmas gifts an EMPTY box that is festively wrapped so your friend can use it next year as decoration. Say it's not empty, it's "filled with love."
- Repurpose thrift store frames to use for your own photos and pictures.

- In your garden, make a decorative pen for your animal statuettes, select potted plants, and any other décor.
- Send packages with touches of interior decorative packaging on top of the usual packing material. Try colored basket shred, silk flower pieces, or colorful ribbons.

- Get a second area rug if you think the pattern is really special because one day—when they're out of stock—you may want both of them in a bigger room or patio where they'll match.
- Flavor your sugar with fresh lavender (after you get a lavender plant) or flavor olive oil with your favorite herbs.

PALOMA'S WWFD LIST

These are my contributions to the WWFD *Little Bits of Joy*:

- Keep decorative and colorful liquor and wine bottles to store the contents of the other less attractive ones.
- Make patio oil lanterns out of your favorite decorative bottles with lantern kits.
- Laminate your favorite calendar pictures or mini posters to make custom placemats, OR glass mount them for wall pictures.
- Get those crystal vases and bowls out of the china cabinet for tea bags, snack bars, colored straws, and bag clips.

- Use cute, emptied jars and containers for candies, nuts, or even pet treats.
- Break out those pretty coasters you never use and repurpose for mini spoon rests, candle holders, or snacks.

🕊 Boil fragrant fruits and spices for a natural potpourri.

- Vigorously shake coffee creamer to make foamy lattes . . . without spending money on a frothier!
- Splash vanilla or almond extract or pumpkin spice in your coffee.

- Use natural jellies as a sweetener for tea.
- Doctor up a plain can of creamed soup with your own broiled veggies and seasonings.
- Use your favorite blender to smooth out your soups "restaurant-style." Add a dollop of sour cream or yogurt.

Acknowledgments

Coming up with an original idea, especially in book form, can expose you to skepticism, criticism, and rejection. Instead of any of that, my friend, Soror (Delta Sigma Theta Sorority, Inc.), Spelman Sister, and fellow September baby, Lisa Bynes, has been my personal cheerleader since I first mentioned *Little Bits of Joy* and other projects to her. That kind of energetic support is what everyone needs to make it through life inside and outside of the traditional "eight to five." She is the catalyst that encourages me to convert my ideas into more than I could have imagined.

My mom and husband are very left-brained, logical people. I thank them for keeping me focused which they know can be a challenge for my creative right brain.

Customer service quality and formats are very frustrating to us in The 50th Dimension, who grew up before dial options, voice prompts, and bot agents. BookLogix still gives twentieth century-level service with twenty-first century skills. They patiently waited months for me to get around to finishing my to-do list tasks for them. They had no judgement in their tone or mannerisms. Their input and sweet professionalism gave me the mental momentum I needed to keep working.

About the Author

I am a sixty-plus-year-old female Datacom professional and sometimes entrepreneur. In 2016, at fifty-six, I coined the phrase The 50th Dimension, after making common observations of myself, family, and friends over fifty. My social media posts and related books contain tips for and expressions of our similar experiences at this time of our lives. This is just one of my right-brained creative outlets used when in-between left-brained technical jobs. It is a good feeling to see my talents in use now. I sure hope it helps make retirement a little easier later.

www.ingramcontent.com/pod-product-compliance
Lightning Source LLC
Chambersburg PA
CBHW071249070526
44583CB00017B/2396